AUSTRALIA'S
PARROTS

Photography by Ken Stepnell
Text by Dalys Newman

WOOLLAHRA

PREVIOUS PAGE: A threatened species, the turquoise parrot *(Neophema pulchella)* is found in areas of south-east Australia. Its favoured habitats are forest, open woodland, savannah with trees and groups of trees along watercourses.

ABOVE: The scarlet-breasted parrot *(Neophema splendida)* is found in the dry mallee and mulga scrubland of southern Australia. During courtship the male perches next to the female, calling loudly and opening his wings and spreading his tail.

BELOW LEFT: Also called the rose-throated parakeet, the princess parrot *(Polytelis alexandrae)* is a rare inhabitant of the arid interior. They are highly nomadic, their movement being governed by the occurrence of ephemeral waters and the flowering of acacias.

BELOW RIGHT: Found in the dry, open areas of the Top End, the hooded parrot *(Psephotus dissimilis)* builds its nest in termite mounds.

OPPOSITE: The female eclectus parrot *(Eclectus roratus)* is predominantly red with a black bill. These parrots have a loud, raucous krraatch-krraak call, repeated three times.

The male eclectus parrot *(Eclectus roratus)* has predominantly green plumage. Mostly seen flying in pairs, these parrots are found in the coastal rainforest areas of Cape York and New Guinea.

TOP: Tropical, lowland birds, varied lorikeets *(Trichoglossus versicolor)* are found in family groups and small flocks in northern Australia. They are the only species of lorikeet with a white ring around their eyes. They are found in all areas with dense tree cover, paperback and eucalypt trees alongside watercourses or around waterholes. They are occasionally seen in large flocks on flowering trees, often alongside red-collared lorikeets. Aggressive feeders, they will drive off honey-eaters and other blossom-feeding species. Swift, direct fliers, they stay very close together and utter shrill, discordant screeches.

ABOVE RIGHT: Also known as the golden-winged parrot, the endangered golden-shouldered parrot *(Psephotus chrysopterygius)* is found in areas of the Northern Territory and Queensland. When courting, the male flies around the female and then perches in front of her with wings slightly opened and head feathers raised to form a small crest. They are usually seen in pairs or family groups.

BELOW: A rare and endangered bird, the orange-bellied parrot *(Neophema chrysogaster)* has breeding sites in the coastal areas of south-west Tasmania and overwinters along the coast of south-east Australia.

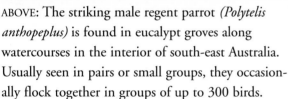

ABOVE: The striking male regent parrot *(Polytelis anthopeplus)* is found in eucalypt groves along watercourses in the interior of south-east Australia. Usually seen in pairs or small groups, they occasionally flock together in groups of up to 300 birds.

ABOVE RIGHT: A shy bird, the elegant parrot *(Neophema elegans)* inhabits open country, coastal sand dunes and cultivated paddocks in south-western and south-eastern Australia. When on the ground, their plumage blends extremely well with the vegetation.

RIGHT: Mallee ringneck parrots *(Barnardius barnardi)* inhabit low eucalyptus scrubland, open woodland and trees along watercourses in the interior of eastern Australia. Five eggs are usually laid in a nest in a hollow limb or hole in a tree and both birds share nest duties. Because of their isolated habitat, encroaching settlement has led to a decline in their numbers.

OPPOSITE: Restricted to south-western Australia, the twenty-eight parrot *(Barnardius zonarius semitorquatus)* is related to the more common Port Lincoln parrot. It is so-named because of its call which resembles the words twenty-eight.

OVERLEAF: Swift parrots *(Lathamus discolor)* are often seen in small flocks feeding on eucalyptus blossom. These migratory parrots breed in Tasmania, returning to the mainland for the winter months.

ABOVE: The naretha bluebonnet *(Psephotus haematogaster narethae)* is found in south-eastern Western Australia and along the edges of the Nullarbor Plains. They appear to have extended their distribution area eastwards in recent decades.

ABOVE RIGHT: Found in the coastal areas of South and Western Australia, the rock parrot *(Neophema petrophila)* has the dullest plumage of its genus. Its preferred habitat is coastal sand dunes and bleak, rocky offshore islets. It is seldom seen more than a few hundred metres inland, occasionally migrating for several kilometres along river estuaries.

CENTRE RIGHT: Often seen nesting in posts and perching on telephone wires, the blue-wing parrot *(Neophema chryso-stoma)* is found in south-eastern Australia and is especially common in Tasmania. Very social, they are generally seen in small flocks, even during the breeding season.

RIGHT: A sub-species of the mallee ringneck parrot, the Cloncurry parrot *(Barnardius barnadi macgillivrayi)* is found in north-western Queensland and the adjacent area of the Northern Territory.

LEFT: The red-browed fig parrot *(Cyclopsitta diophthalma macleayana)* is one of three different species of fig parrot in Australia. It is found mainly along the coastal areas of northern Queensland. Their diet is made up of fruits, particularly figs and berries, seeds, nectar, insects and larvae. In flight, they have a shrill penetrating call, but when feeding they are usually silent. Small, stocky parrots, they have extremely short, rounded tails and red foreheads. The female has duller, more yellowish plumage than the male.

BELOW: Mainly found in New South Wales and Victoria, the superb parrot *(Polytelis swainsonii)* can sometimes be seen on harvested fields, foraging for grain. Active during the early morning and late afternoon, they are usually seen on the ground searching for seeds or in the treetops feeding on blossoms. They nest in holes in the treetops or in hollow branches of eucalypts along watercourses. Nests are lined with pieces of rotten wood and four to six eggs are laid.

OPPOSITE, BELOW AND RIGHT: The highly colourful red-winged parrot *(Aprosmictus erythropterus)* is found in northern and north-eastern Australia and southern New Guinea. They are regular visitors to grain-growing areas and inhabit open eucalypt forest, acacia and casuarina groves along rocky ridges. Arboreal, they come down to the ground only to drink, feeding on fruits, berries, nuts, seeds, flowers, nectar, insects and insect larvae found in trees and bushes. They are occasionally seen in flocks with pale-headed rosellas and mallee ring-neck parrots, but usually they travel in pairs or small family groups. The female (right) has dull green plumage with restricted red markings. She nests in a hollow limb or hole in a tree, laying up to six eggs.

BELOW RIGHT: A nomadic bird of semi-arid country, the Bourke's parrot *(Neophema bourkii)* is found in inland southern and central Australia. An inhabitant of dry acacia scrubland, it is quiet and tame and usually seen in pairs or small groups.

BOTTOM RIGHT: Mulga parrots *(Psephotus varius)* are found in the interior of southern Australia, inhabiting grasslands, arid scrublands and groves of mulga, myall or stunted eucalypts. Most of these trees are small and stunted, so nesting hollows are usually badly formed and close to the ground.

OPPOSITE: The red-vented bluebonnet *(Psephotus haematorrhous)* is found in southern Queensland and northern New South Wales. Bluebonnets are fairly common in inland areas and are often seen around farm buildings and stock-watering troughs.

ABOVE: Port Lincoln parrots *(Barnardius zonarius)* range throughout areas of Western Australia, South Australia and the Northern Territory. A very successful species, it is found in a wide range of habitats throughout more than a third of the continent and is extremely abundant in the wheat belt of Western Australia.

BELOW: Spending much of their day feeding among eucalypt branches, the red-capped parrot *(Purpureicephalus spurius)* is found only in south-western Western Australia. These parrots frequent marri forests and trees surrounding cultivated farmlands or bordering roads and watercourses; they also visit parklands and orchards.

ABOVE AND CENTRE: The brilliantly coloured king parrot *(Alisterus scapularis)* inhabits forest and open woodland along the east coast of Australia. Usually found in small groups, they feed both on the ground and in trees on seeds, fruits, berries, nectar and leaf buds. The males have scarlet heads and bodies and dark green wings banded with pale green. Females (centre) are mostly dark green with a red belly.

BELOW: Found in all types of terrain with tree cover, the red-collared lorikeet *(Trichoglossus haematodus rubritorquis)* is commonly seen actively climbing among the branches. It is related to the rainbow lorikeet and is a conspicuous and noisy bird, with a shrill call.

OPPOSITE: Rainbow lorikeets *(Trichoglossus haematodus)* are noisy, fast-flying parrots found in east and south-eastern Australia as far as Eyre Peninsula and Kangaroo Island. Like other lorikeets, they have brush-like tongues adapted for gathering nectar and pollen.

LEFT AND BELOW: Red-rumped parrots *(Psephotus haematonotus)* are found in grasslands and open plains in south-east Australia, north-east South Australia and south-west Queensland. They are seldom found far from water and are also a common sight on golfcourses, playing fields, farm yards and suburban allotments. Friendly birds, they will walk or waddle away when encountered rather than take flight. They have a distinctive pretty warbling call, unusual for a parrot, and when in flight they utter a cheery 'chee-chip, chee-chip'. Nests are built in tree hollows, fence posts or hollow stumps and four to six, white, rounded eggs are laid. They are often seen at rest in foliage during the heat of the day and they feed on eucalypt and other blossom, spilt grain on roadsides and in fowlyards. The male parrot (below) has much brighter plumage than the predominantly olive-green female (left).

ABOVE LEFT: Purple-crowned lorikeets *(Glossopsitta porphy-rocephala)* are nomadic, following the flowering eucalypts for their food requirements. An inland species, they inhabit drier, lightly timbered country in south-western and south-eastern Australia.

ABOVE RIGHT: The little lorikeet *(Glossopsitta pusilla)* grows to 15 centimetres and is found in eastern and south-eastern Australia. Occurring at all altitudes, they are common in wooded country wherever there are flowering or fruit-bearing trees and shrubs.

LEFT: Mainly a lowland bird, the scaly-breasted lorikeet *(Trichoglossus chlorolepidotus)* is particularly common in the north-east of Australia. These noisy parrots are often seen in flocks flying high overhead or in the outermost branches of flowering eucalypts. Greedy feeders, they climb along twigs to get at flowers, often hanging upside down to reach them.

TOP LEFT: The cockatiel *(Nymphicus hollandicus)* is the only small Australian parrot with a crest. Often seen in small flocks, these birds are distributed throughout the interior of Australia, inhabiting most types of open country close to water. They can be a pest in grain-growing areas, where they often cause considerable damage. Both parents share nest duties and the young birds leave the nest at five weeks old.

LEFT: Often seen roosting in pairs, the musk lorikeet *(Glossopitta concinna)* is an extremely noisy bird, its presence announced by continuous screeching. They are found throughout eastern and south-eastern Australia, including Tasmania and Kangaroo Island.

LEFT: Popular world-wide as cage birds, budgerigars *(Melopsittacus undulates)* are the most abundant of Australian parrots. Found throughout the continent, but not in Tasmania, they are extremely nomadic, their movements dependant on the availability of water and seeding grasses. The flock flies with outstanding precision, twisting and turning as one. The flocks can be of legendary size in the interior during favourable years, darkening the sky with their numbers.

LEFT AND OPPOSITE: Golden-mantled rosellas *(Platycercus eximinus cecilae)* are a sub-species of the eastern rosella. Found in south-east Queensland and north-east New South Wales, their heads and breasts are a darker red than the eastern rosella and their back and wing feathers have rich golden edging. They are troublesome in orchards and they are often seen visiting stubble paddocks after harvesting to feed on fallen grain. The female bird (left) has less extensive and duller red markings on her head than the male (opposite).

OPPOSITE: The pale-headed rosella *(Platycercus adscitus)* has a white, yellow-tinged head with violet-blue and white cheek patches. Lowland birds, they inhabit most types of timbered country in areas of Queensland and New South Wales. The mottled colouring on their backs blends well with grass coverage, giving good camouflage.

TOP RIGHT: The colourful eastern rosella *(Platycercus eximius)* lays up to nine eggs, usually in a hollow limb. The young birds remain with their parents for many months after leaving the nest. They are often seen in the outer branches of tall eucalypts, preening and chewing on the tree limbs.

RIGHT: Found in coastal and adjacent areas in south-west Australia from Moore River to Albany, the western rosella *(Platycercus icterotis)* is the smallest of the species. It is usually found in pairs and small family groups, with several groups gathering together at harvest time to forage for grain.

RIGHT AND BOTTOM RIGHT: Also called the red lowry, the crimson rosella *(Platycercus elegans)* is one of the best known of the rosella family. Found in areas of Victoria, South Australia, Queensland and New South Wales, small groups are often seen feeding on the ground in the suburbs. Male birds (below) have rich crimson plumage with violet-blue cheek patches. The immature birds (right) congregate in nomadic flocks after the breeding season and do not attain their adult plumage until sixteen months old.

OVERLEAF: King parrots *(Alisterus scapularis)* are found in eastern Australia from southern Victoria to northern Queensland, but their habitat has been reduced by the replacement of eucalypts with conifer plantations. The male bird is brilliant in colour compared to the predominantly green female. They have a heavy, deliberate flight with rhythmic wingbeats and are not as noisy or active as most other parrots. On the ground they walk with an awkward, waddling gait.

ABOVE: The northern rosella *(Platycercus venustus)* is found in north-western and northern Australia from the Kimberleys east to the Northern Territory–Queensland border. Pairs or groups of up to eight birds can be seen in the treetops or on the ground foraging for seeds. They fly swiftly, staying close to the ground, gliding up into trees and fanning their tails before alighting.

BELOW LEFT: The Adelaide rosella *(Platycercus elegans adelaidae)* is found in a very restricted area in southern South Australia from the southern Flinders Ranges to the Fleurieu Peninsula south of Adelaide. It inhabits all types of timbered country and is often seen in suburban gardens and parkland in Adelaide.

BELOW LEFT: Found only in Tasmania and the larger Bass Strait islands, green rosellas *(Platycercus caledonicus)* are often seen in flocks with Tasmanian rosellas. They inhabit forest, savannah with trees, heathland, pasture, orchards, parks and gardens.

OPPOSITE: The largest parrot in Australia, the palm cockatoo *(Probosciger atterimus)* reaches a length of 60 centimetres. It is only found on the tip of the Cape York Peninsula, where their size, black colouring and piercing alarm call make them very conspicuous.

Often seen feasting on banksia cones, the yellow-tailed black cockatoo *(Calyptorhynchus funereus funereus)* is found in areas of Victoria, South Australia, New South Wales, Queensland and Tasmania. Noisy, conspicuous birds, they mainly inhabit wet coastal woodlands.

ABOVE: Found mostly in northern Australia, the red-tailed cockatoos *(Calyptorhynchus magnificus)* have loud raucous cries, particularly when alarmed. They can often be seen flying about on moonlit nights.

CENTRE RIGHT: Gang gang cockatoos *(Callocephalon fimbriatum)* are arboreal, coming to the ground only to drink or to examine fallen nuts or cones. During the heat of the day they often sit motionless for hours at a time or engage in mutual preening. They inhabit mountain forests and wooded valleys, and are most plentiful in southern New South Wales and eastern Victoria.

BOTTOM RIGHT: The bare-eyed corella *(Cacatua tenuirostris pastinator)* is a sub-species of the long-billed corella found in south-west Australia. Fairly uncommon, it is only found in two small populations which are recovering in numbers because of statutory protection.

ABOVE: The white-tailed black cockatoo *(Calyptorhynchus funereus baudinii)* is found in the heavily forested area in the extreme south-west corner of Western Australia, where the rainfall is 750 millimetres or greater. Marri seeds and insect larvae are their favoured food and they are also known to raid apple orchards, stripping fruit to get at the seeds.

LEFT: Sulphur-crested cockatoos *(Cacatua galerita)* have, along with galahs, become serious agricultural pests in some wheat and oil-seed growing areas. Found in northern and eastern Australia, they are one of the country's best known birds.

LEFT: One of the most numerous and wide-spread of Australia's parrots, galahs *(Cacatua roseicapilla)* are found throughout the country. They do not breed until they are four years old and pairs mate for life, usually using the same nest site each year.

OPPOSITE: Also called the pink cockatoo, the Major Mitchell's cockatoo *(Cacatua leadbeateri)* is found in the interior of Australia, apart from the north-eastern regions. They are usually seen in pairs or small groups, often alongside galahs and little corellas.

LEFT: Long-billed corellas *(Cacatua tenuirostris)* are found in the higher rainfall areas of southern Australia. They are a declining species due to increasing aridity and land-clearance. Seldom found far from water, they visit waterholes to drink at dusk and well before sunrise. A favourite food is the corms of onion weed, which the birds dig up with their elongated beaks.

BELOW: Little corellas *(Cacatua sanguinea)* are found through-out the interior of eastern Australia, north-western and northern Australia, including the off-shore islands. Conspicuous birds, they are usually found in flocks of several hundred to thousands in number, often occupying trees so densely that the leaves appear to be white. When large flocks are feeding on the ground, all birds move along in the same direction, with those at the back continually rising and flying up to the front. They inhabit open woodland, mangrove areas, cultivated areas and are also found in towns, gardens and parklands.